# CLOSET DESIGN

# BIBLE

**ORO**
**EDITIONS**

Publishers of Architecture, Art, and Design
Gordon Goff: Publisher

www.oroeditions.com
info@oroeditions.com

Published by ORO Editions

Graphic Design: Drew Evans, LA Closet Design
Text: LA Closet Design
ORO Project Coordinator: Kirby Anderson

10 9 8 7 6 5 4 3 2 1 First Edition

Library of Congress data available upon request. World Rights: Available

ISBN: 978-1-940743-44-8

Color Separations and Printing: ORO Group Ltd.
Printed in China.

International Distribution: www.oroeditions.com/distribution

ORO Editions makes a continuous effort to minimize the overall carbon footprint of its publications. As part of this goal, ORO Editions, in association with Global ReLeaf, arranges to plant trees to replace those used in the manufacturing of the paper produced for its books. Global ReLeaf is an international campaign run by American Forests, one of the world's oldest nonprofit conservation organizations. Global ReLeaf is American Forests' education and action program that helps individuals, organizations, agencies, and corporations improve the local and global environment by planting and caring for trees.

*TO CALM THE CHAOS OF EVERYDAY LIFE*

*lisa adams*

# LUXURY. CALM. SANCTUARY.

LISA ADAMS is the creative force behind LA Closet Design, a full service firm offering personalized dressing spaces to calm the chaos of everyday living. Lisa's vision goes beyond functionality – her wardrobes are balanced, luxurious sanctuaries that combine a timeless attention to detail with a modern focus on environmentally harmonious materials. As a result, she creates spaces that reflect a unique blend of sophistication and accessibility.

Born and raised in Honolulu, Lisa holds two Graduate Degrees and an MBA from Pepperdine University. In her career, she has created spaces for a notable client base including Christina Aguilera, Reese Witherspoon, Billy Crystal, Tyra Banks, Khloe Kardashian, and Kris Jenner. The launch of LA Closet Design has given Lisa the opportunity to expand her design expertise and aesthetic vision, taking customized wardrobe spaces from concept to completion.

| | | |
|---|---|---|
| **1** THE FASHION FORWARD CLOSET | **2** THE DESIGNER'S CLOSET | **3** THE DAPPER DRESSING ROOM |
| **7** THE COASTAL CLOSET | **8** THE BOUTIQUE CLOSET | **9** THE TAILORED DRESSING ROOM |
| **13** THE MODERN GLAM CLOSET | **14** THE CHIC SHOPPER'S CLOSET | **15** THE DARK ROOM |

**4** THE ELEGANT EAST COAST CLOSET

**5** THE ESQUIRE CLOSET

**6** THE FRENCH MANOR CLOSET

**10** THE LONDON LOFT CLOSET

**11** THE DISPLAY BOUTIQUE

**12** THE CLASSIC WHITE CLOSET

**16** THE WEST COAST WORKOUT CLOSET

**17** THE MAN CAVE CLOSET

**18** THE NURSERY CLOSET

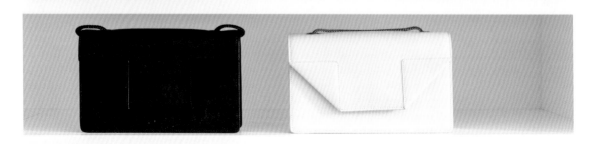

# 1

# THE
# FASHION
# FORWARD
# CLOSET

# TIP

BOOT TREES MAKE FOR A MORE
BOUTIQUE APPEARANCE, AND HELP
BOOTS KEEP THEIR SHAPE.

# THE DESIGNER'S CLOSET

# 3

# THE
# DAPPER
# DRESSING
# ROOM

INSTALL A TOWEL ROD FOR
HANGING TIES AND SCARVES.

# THE
# ELEGANT
# EAST COAST
# CLOSET

29

# TIP

DISPLAY SHOES AND ACCESSORIES
WITH PROPER LIGHTING.

# THE
# ESQUIRE
# CLOSET

# TIP

INCORPORATE A MIRROR TO
VISUALLY EXPAND THE SPACE AND
EASE THE DRESSING PROCESS.

# THE
# FRENCH
# MANOR
# CLOSET

# TIP

PURSE HOOKS PROTECT YOUR BAGS,
AND KEEP THEM FROM PILING UP ON
A SHELF.

# THE
# COASTAL
# CLOSET

TIP

STORE SCARVES MORE EFFICIENTLY
IN A PULL-OUT CABINET.

# THE
# BOUTIQUE
# CLOSET

A PULL-OUT RACK KEEPS PANTS
VISIBLE AND NEATLY FOLDED.

# THE TAILORED DRESSING ROOM

# TIP

KEEP YOUR HANGERS CONSISTENT
FOR A CLEANER LOOK.

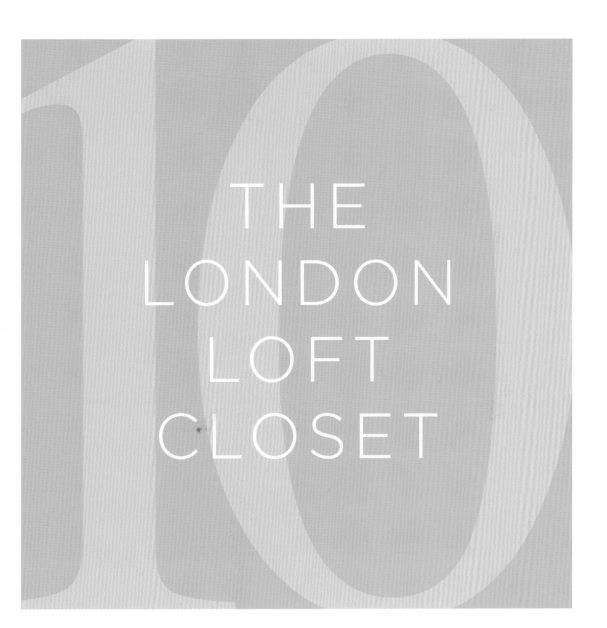

# THE
# LONDON
# LOFT
# CLOSET

# TIP

UTILIZE THE FULL HEIGHT OF YOUR
SPACE FOR STORAGE.

# 11

# THE
# DISPLAY
# BOUTIQUE

CUSTOM DRAWER INSERTS KEEP
SUNGLASSES AND JEWELRY
ORGANIZED AND ACCESSIBLE.

# THE
# CLASSIC
# WHITE
# CLOSET

BRING YOUR HAMPERS AND IRONING
BOARD INTO THE CLOSET.

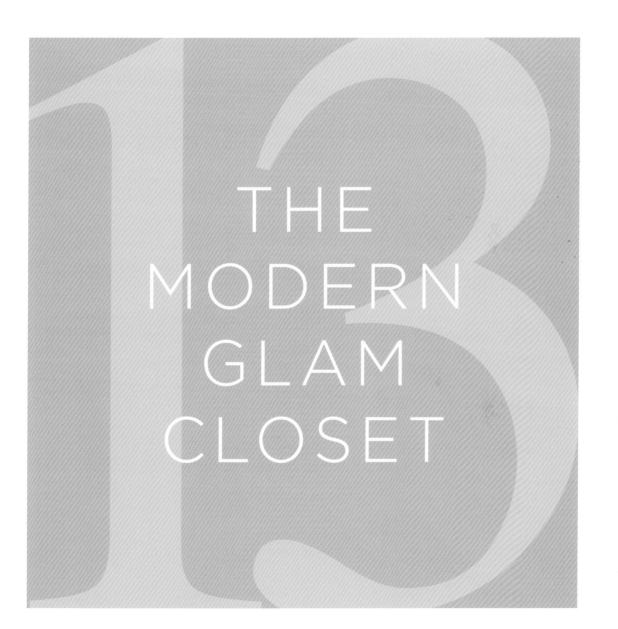

# 13

## THE MODERN GLAM CLOSET

# TIP

INCORPORATE A VANITY TO KEEP
BEAUTY PRODUCTS ORGANIZED.

# THE
# CHIC
# SHOPPER'S
# CLOSET

# TIP

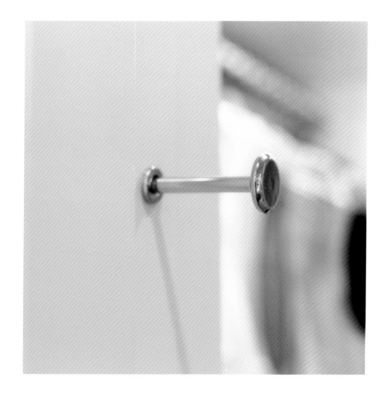

INCORPORATE PULL-OUT VALET
HOOKS FOR STAGING.

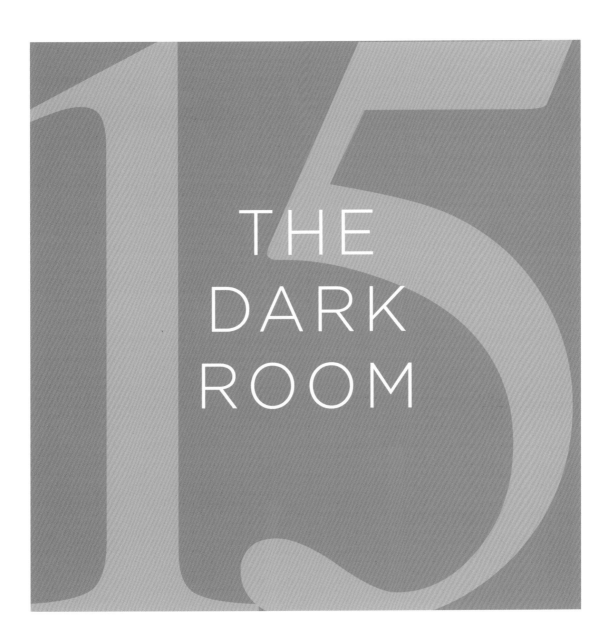

# 15

## THE DARK ROOM

KEEP DEVICES OUT OF SIGHT AND POWERED UP
WITH A CHARGING DRAWER.

# THE
# WEST COAST
# WORKOUT
# CLOSET

# TIP

A GLASS DISPLAY IS A GREAT WAY
TO SHOWCASE ACCESSORIES AND
KEEP THEM DUST FREE.

# THE
# MAN CAVE
# CLOSET

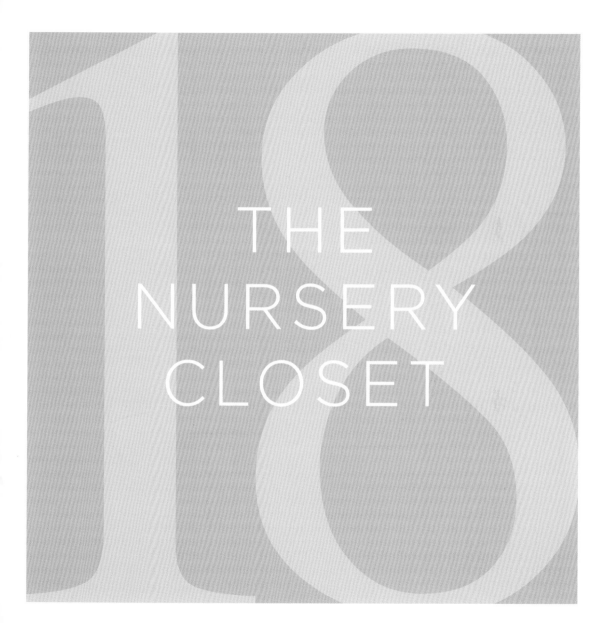

# THE
# NURSERY
# CLOSET

FAMILY
FOREVER

endure

WRITE IT ON
YOUR HEART
THAT EVERY
DAY IS THE
BEST DAY OF
YOUR LIFE.

# CLIENTS